THE CARIBBEAN
AND ITS PEOPLE

T. W. Mayer

Thomson Learning
New York

PEOPLE
· AND PLACES ·

Title page: Schoolchildren from the Virgin Islands pose for a photo taken outside their schoolroom.

Contents page: Two women from the Bahamas stop to have their picture taken on the way to the market.

Consultant: Dr. Tony Binns, lecturer in geography at the University of Sussex, England.

First published in the United States in 1995 by
Thomson Learning
115 Fifth Avenue
New York, NY 10003

Published simultaneously in Great Britain by
Wayland (Publishers) Ltd.

Library of Congress Cataloging-in-Publication Data
Mayer, T. W.
   The Caribbean and its people / T.W. Mayer.
       p.   cm.—(People and places)
   Includes bibliographical references and index.
   ISBN 1-56847-338-9
   1. West Indies—Juvenile literature. 2. Caribbean Area—Juvenile
literature. [1. West Indies. 2. Caribbean Area.] I. Title. II Series.
F1608.3.M39   1995
972.9—dc20   94-34824

Printed in Italy

Acknowledgments
The publishers would like to thank the following for allowing their photographs to be reproduced in this book:
Action Plus 33; AKG 15; Bridgeman 24; Camera Press 26; J. A. Cash 16-17, 28; Cephas 32; Coleman 6-7; Eye Ubiquitous 9, 18 (top), 19, 37; Harding 6, 27, 34, 38; Hutchison 31, 39, 44; J. & P. Hubley 22, 42; Life File 21 (right); Mary Evans 20, 21 (left), 22-23; NHPA 8; Photri 4, 25 (top), 25 (bottom), 35; Rex 29 (top); Tony Stone Images 1, 12, 13, 30, 40, 41, 45; Wayland 18 (bottom), 29 (bottom); Zefa 3, 10-11, 36, 43.
All artwork by Peter Bull.

C O N T E N T S

·INTRODUCTION·

The English writer Charles Kingsley wrote this of the islands of the Caribbean:

One fancies, at moments, that the islands do not rise up out of the sea, but float upon it; that they are held in place, not by the roots of the mountains, and deep miles of lava wall below, but by the cloud which has caught them by the top, and will not let them go.

Grand Piton, St. Lucia. The flat land is thick with vegetation, but few plants can cling to the steep hillside.

The islands *are* actually the tips of undersea mountains that stretch away from the mainland of the U.S. before they curve back to meet the mainland of South America, off the coast of Venezuela. They were created by volcanic activity deep in the earth, as plates of land ground against each other. This caused the edges of the plates to rise up, creating a chain of islands around the edge of the Caribbean Sea.

The Caribbean is a true melting pot, into which many different peoples have been poured and mixed together. Its many cultures make it one of the world's most fascinating places to visit. The Arawak Indians, who were among the first inhabitants, were followed from South America by the fierce Caribs. Next came Spanish, English, French, and other Europeans, exploring and then settling the region. The Europeans brought slaves from western Africa to work on sugar and tobacco plantations. After slavery was abolished, the slaves' jobs were done by workers from China and India. In the twentieth century, Lebanese, Syrians, and others have moved to the Caribbean. These peoples have given something of themselves to the region and its ways of life. Music, cooking, clear skies and seas, and the warmth of the climate and people all mark the Caribbean as a very special place.

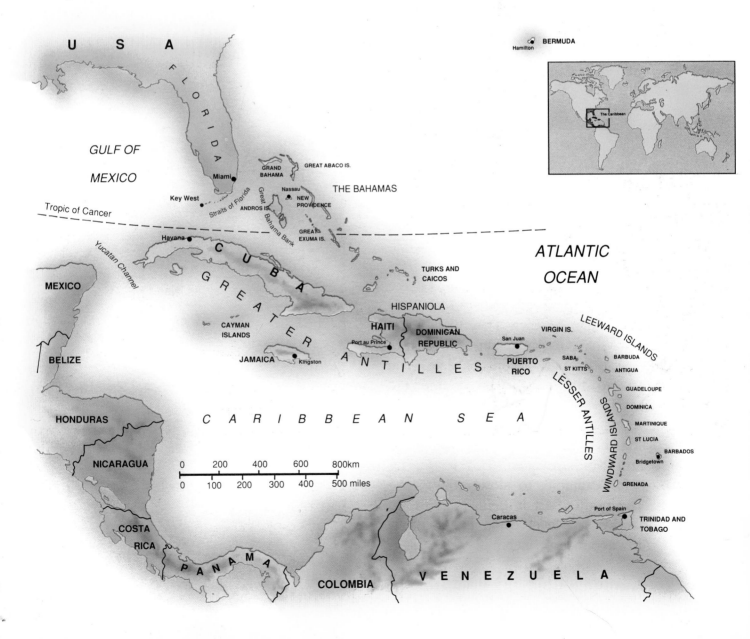

"The island came out of the sea …In the beginning they were solitary isles really. Then the isles turned into mountains and the shallows in between them became valleys. Later the islands joined to form a bigger island which soon was green where it wasn't reddish or brown. The island was a haven for birds and for fish but it was never any good for mammals. There's the island, still coming out between the sea and the gulf, garlanded by keys and cays and fastened by the stream to the ocean. There it is …"
(*A View of Dawn in the Tropics*, G. Cabrera Infante.)

The thickly wooded north coast of Trinidad drops steeply into the sea. (Inset) Hot springs on St. Lucia, caused by geothermal energy, rise to the surface.

The oldest rocks and mountains in the Caribbean are in the Greater Antilles, which are made up of the islands Jamaica, Hispaniola, and Puerto Rico. These islands were first pushed up out of the sea by volcanic activity under the seabed, 70 million years ago. There are no live volcanoes there now. Farther south and east, along the line of the Windward Islands, there are still volcanoes, and earthquakes when the earth shifts its balance far below the surface.

Most of the Caribbean islands lie on the edge of an underground plate which they share with Central America. They were created when this plate moved against the edge of the North and South American plate. The movement to the north that created the Greater Antilles is now finished, but, even so, these islands are still changing their shape. The plate is now moving eastward and grinding against North America. This is causing Jamaica, for example, to slowly tilt to the south. The north coast is being pushed up further above sea level while the south is being drowned inch by inch.

There are active volcanoes on the islands of St. Vincent and Guadeloupe in the Lesser Antilles. Martinique's capital, St. Pierre, was wiped out by an eruption of Mt. Pelée on May 8, 1902. North of Grenada is an undersea volcano with the unusual name of "Kick 'em Jenny." On many of the Windward islands, and some of the Leewards, there are old volcanic craters and hot springs. On St. Lucia, one of the most popular places for tourists to visit, is a volcano called Soufrière, where it is possible to drive into the crater. The volcano smells of sulfur and gets its name from the French word for sulfur. On Dominica is a famous "boiling lake," which is heated by geothermal energy from deep beneath the surface of the earth. Because these islands lie along a fault line that is still active, the threat of a volcanic eruption looms over the people who live on them.

▲
Bats, the only Caribbean mammals that can fly between islands, are common.

Cuba and the Bahamas are both part of the North American plate and are plates of limestone. Southern Cuba lies right on the edge of the North American plate. This causes the countryside there to be hilly.

Trinidad and Tobago were once joined to South America. When the Ice Age ended and the sea level rose, they were cut off from the mainland and became part of the necklace of islands of the Caribbean.

WILDLIFE

Except for bats, there are very few mammals in the Caribbean, apart from those in Trinidad and Tobago. Bats can fly between the islands and are common throughout the islands. When Trinidad and Tobago were part of South America, many mammals were trapped there when the sea cut the islands off from the mainland. The two islands have howler monkeys, weeping capuchins, brown forest deer, opossums, and armadillo, and more than 50 kinds of bats.

There are many different kinds of birds in the Caribbean: some live on the islands, and others pass through on their migrations. Bird-watching tourists come to the islands in the hope of spotting a rare species, such as a Grenada dove or a Guadeloupe woodpecker. Trinidad is home to South American and Caribbean birds. The island's Asa Wright Center is a very famous bird-watching location. The flamingo is one of the most distinctive birds in the world. The world's largest group of flamingoes is at Lake Windsor on the island of Little Inagua in the Bahamas. The island of Bonaire, in the southern Caribbean, has a big flamingo colony, too.

What sounds like one of the Caribbean's less glamorous birds—the Dominican mountain chicken—is not actually a bird at all, but a frog. It gets its name from the way it tastes when cooked. Cuba is home to the world's smallest frog, the Cuban pygmy frog.

There are many different turtles in the Caribbean. Female sea turtles come ashore between May and August to lay their eggs in the sandy beaches. Turtle eggs and the turtles themselves have been part of the Caribbean diet for years. The ever-increasing numbers of visitors to the islands want to try traditional foods. Turtles are high on their list of things to taste. Recently, too many of them have been caught, so some kinds of turtles are now protected by law. There is a large commercial farm for breeding for green sea turtles in the Cayman Islands, which has helped to ease the pressure on wild turtles. Restaurants can buy commercially bred turtles instead of ones that have been caught in the ocean.

A young visitor to the Grand Cayman turtle farm gets a close look at one of the locals. Turtles are a popular food in the Caribbean, so turtle farms can make a lot of money.

There are snakes on many of the islands, although few are really dangerous. The exception is the fer de lance snake, which is found on the islands of Martinique, St. Lucia, Trinidad, and Tobago. Although its bite can send you to the hospital, it is rarely fatal. St. Lucia has set up the Marias Islands Nature Reserve to protect its rare creatures, which include the fer de lance, ground lizards, and a very rare grass snake—there may be no more than 150 of these left.

Some of the most interesting creatures are those that have been introduced to the islands by people. To fight the poisonous snakes, European settlers who had been to India brought mongooses to the islands. They have spread everywhere. Mongooses eat any small birds and animals, and, as a result, the ground parrots that used to be common in the Caribbean have become increasingly rare. So have other birds, reptiles, and small animals.

A diver in The Bahamas swims with a friendly dolphin. The seas of the Caribbean are full of life. This, and the clear water, brings divers to the area from all round the world.

Marine toads were introduced to try and reduce the number of insects, such as mosquitoes, that make pests of themselves. Unfortunately for the toads, during the mating season, the males use the flat surfaces of the roads to show off to prospective mates, and end up being squashed.

The rain forests of the Greater Antilles contain black widow spiders, which can give a poisonous bite if they are surprised or frightened. In the Lesser Antilles, the rain forests hold the less dangerous but still quite startling Hercules beetle, which can grow as long as four and one-half inches long.

The seas of the Caribbean are rich in marine life. Many of the islands have coral reefs that attract all kinds of fish, as well as divers from all over the world. Divers come to see grunts, butterflies, soldier, and angel fish, and to watch the barracuda hovering almost motionless, looking for prey. They try to avoid the tiny damsel fish, which guard their territory so fiercely that they will even attack humans. Fortunately, their mouths are too small for them to do any harm. Other dangerous sea creatures include moray eels, sharks, and poisonous scorpion fish.

The reefs are made of many varieties of coral, which can be seen either by diving or by traveling in a glass-bottomed boat. Avoid touching the fire coral, which comes in several different shapes but is always recognizable by its white furry tips. Fire coral can give a nasty sting that causes a painful rash.

— El Yunque —

El Yunque forest on Puerto Rico is a magnet for tourists. The forest's official name is the Caribbean National Forest. There are over 240 different kinds of trees, rare wild orchids, bamboos, and giant ferns. The forest is divided into four main zones, each of which overlaps its neighbor: rain forest; thicket; palms; and, high up where the air is thin, dwarf forest.

In 1989 the forest was badly damaged by Hurricane Hugo. Some estimates say the forest will not be back to normal for 15 years. In fact, there have been tropical storms and hurricanes in the region for many centuries. They are part of the natural life of the forests. Hugo wiped out almost the whole population of Puerto Rican parrots. These were once common Rican parrots. These were once common around the picnic areas, where they scavenged for leftover crumbs, but now they are rarely seen.

A party of tourists is guided around El Yunque forest in Puerto Rico.

FORESTS

Many of the Caribbean islands have rain forests, which contain boa constrictors, opposums, hummingbirds, thrashers, toads, parrots, as well as many wonderful flowers. The most beautiful are the orchids and bromeliads. The forests have not suffered from commercial logging in the way that rain forests in South America and Southeast Asia have, although valuable trees have been cut down. Some of these—blue mahoe, balata, and gommier—have become increasingly rare, because like all hardwood trees they take a long time to grow back. The pressure on the natural forests has been eased by commercial plantations of blue mahoe, Caribbean pine, mahogany, and teak.

There are still large areas of rain forest on Martinique, especially at Piton du Carbet, and there are cloud forests on the slopes of Martinique's volcano, Mt. Pelée. On Guadeloupe there are small patches of rain forest where no trees have ever been cut down. This is very unusual in the Caribbean.

Closer to the coasts, the forests change their character. They are mostly dry, scrubby woodland with far less lush vegetation. Some of the trees lose their leaves during the dry season. One of the most recognizable of these is the turpentine tree. Many of the local people call this the "tourist tree," because of its red, peeling bark.

A small cove on the coast of St. Thomas, U.S. Virgin Islands. The forest comes right down to the seashore.

· EARLY HISTORY ·

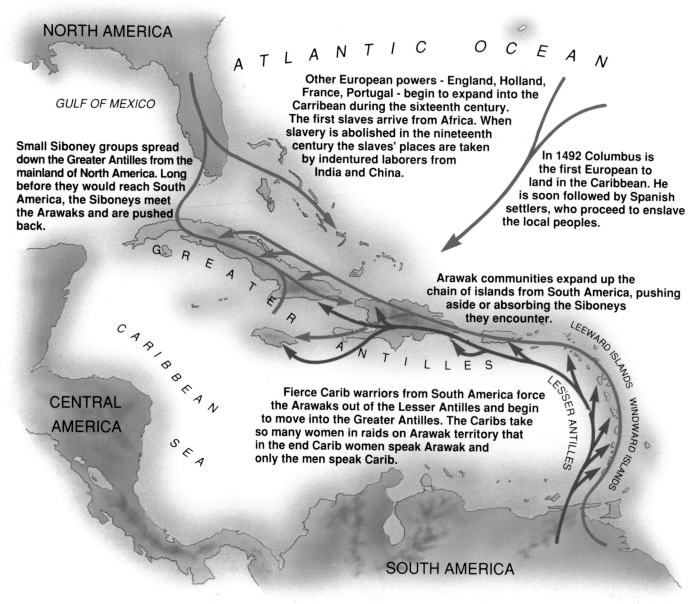

NORTH AMERICA

ATLANTIC OCEAN

GULF OF MEXICO

Small Siboney groups spread down the Greater Antilles from the mainland of North America. Long before they would reach South America, the Siboneys meet the Arawaks and are pushed back.

Other European powers - England, Holland, France, Portugal - begin to expand into the Caribbean during the sixteenth century. The first slaves arrive from Africa. When slavery is abolished in the nineteenth century the slaves' places are taken by indentured laborers from India and China.

In 1492 Columbus is the first European to land in the Caribbean. He is soon followed by Spanish settlers, who proceed to enslave the local peoples.

GREATER ANTILLES

CARIBBEAN SEA

CENTRAL AMERICA

Arawak communities expand up the chain of islands from South America, pushing aside or absorbing the Siboneys they encounter.

LEEWARD ISLANDS

LESSER ANTILLES

WINDWARD ISLANDS

Fierce Carib warriors from South America force the Arawaks out of the Lesser Antilles and begin to move into the Greater Antilles. The Caribs take so many women in raids on Arawak territory that in the end Carib women speak Arawak and only the men speak Carib.

SOUTH AMERICA

"*History begins*" said Fernando Portuondo, "*with the arrival of the white man, whose deeds it records.*" In fact, the history of the Caribbean stretches back many hundreds of years before the arrival of the first Europeans on its shores. No one can be sure of exact dates, because no written records exist, but archaeologists have pieced together much of the early history of the region.

THE SIBONEYS
The first people to settle the islands came from the mainland of North America. The Siboneys, as these people are now known, lived a simple life in small groups beside the shore, or on the banks of streams and rivers. Their communities were small—the biggest archaeologists have ever found was in Cuba and had only about 100 people living in it.

The Siboneys lived off the land, hunting small animals, reptiles, and birds, and gathering wild plants. They never planted any crops of their own, and they never discovered the secret of making metal. Their tools were made of stone, bone, or wood.

THE ARAWAKS

The Arawaks, the next group of people to come to the Caribbean, came slowly over the years from the south, moving from one island to the next. By the time Columbus arrived in 1492, they had spread all through the Caribbean, absorbing or pushing out the Siboneys as they went. Unlike the Siboneys, the Arawaks planted crops. As they expanded to other islands, they developed their skills at shipbuilding and fishing. The Arawaks were tall, healthy people who lived long lives. As many as five hundred thousand of them may have lived on the island of Hispaniola alone.

A 1792 European painting of what Caribbean Indians were thought to look like. The Indians probably did tattoo themselves, but without a clear idea of how the tattoos appeared in real life, the artist has had to guess how they looked.

THE CARIBS

After the Arawaks, the Caribs came to the Caribbean from South America, using Trinidad as their stepping stone. The Caribs' lifestyle was similar to that of the Arawaks, but they depended more on fishing, so most of their settlements were close to the sea. They were a fierce people, and by 1492 they had spread all the way to Puerto Rico, having pushed the Arawaks out of the Lesser Antilles. Their raids on Arawak territory were feared: the Caribs stole the women and took them to work in the fields. In the end, they stole so many women in raids that it became common for Carib warriors to have more than one wife.

When Columbus arrived, he was given a friendly welcome by the Arawaks, who told him and his sailors stories of the fierce cannibals who lived on the islands to the south. There is no evidence of the Caribs being cannibals, but both they and the Arawaks probably made human sacrifices. In any case, after a few encounters the Spaniards left the Caribs alone, discouraged from making contact by their frightening reputation.

THE INDIANS ARE DESTROYED

Wherever they went in South America, the Spaniards were to take people prisoner and force them to work as slaves. The Caribbean was no exception. The Spanish had guns, metal swords, and armor. They were able to force the Arawak villages to pay them tributes in crops and anything else of value that the tribes had. At the same time, the Spanish allowed their herds of pigs and cattle to trample on the unfenced Arawak fields and eat the crops.

The Spanish also started mining for gold using slave labor. This led to many people being transported to areas in which there were not enough crops to feed them, and people began to starve.

As the Arawaks died out, the Spanish began to make slave raids on the Caribs. Like the Arawaks, they were quickly wiped out by murder, work, starvation, or suicide. Many of

the villagers, feeling that they had been deserted by their gods and there was nowhere for them to run, committed mass suicide. It was the only way they could escape.

Today there are no full-blooded Arawak people on the islands of the Caribbean, and only a very few Caribs left on the island of Dominica in the Lesser Antilles.

One of the few remaining descendants of the Carib Indians, after whom the Caribbean is named, with firewood balanced on her head. Almost all the remaining Caribs live on Dominica, where this picture was taken.

A luxurious home in Kingston, Jamaica, built in colonial times.

Frightened slaves are auctioned after a terrible journey from Africa.

▼

The effects of the slave system are still being felt in the Caribbean today. Cuba, then governed by Spain, abolished slavery in 1886. Most other islands had been free of slavery for 50 years by then.

The legacy of slavery can be seen in the environment, where vast areas of land were cleared to make way for single-crop plantations. The islands' economies are still largely trapped in a cycle of selling cheap raw materials, but having to buy expensive manufactured goods from aboard. This is little different from the days of slavery, when sugar and tobacco were among the crops sold abroad to pay for manufactured luxuries.

An old slave house in St. Andrew, Barbados, looks cramped and uncomfortable compared with the merchant's house on the opposite page.

THE PLANTATIONS

Between 1492 and the 1950s, European powers occupied the islands of the Caribbean for profit. By the second half of the seventeenth century, the plantation system had been established. Slave labor, mainly from West Africa, was used to grow single crops, such as sugar. These crops were then exported to Europe or North America and sold. The profits were used to buy more slaves in West Africa. These slaves were then shipped across the Atlantic to be sold in the Caribbean or North America. Much of the profit from this triangular trade ended up in the British ports of Bristol, London, and Liverpool, where it was used to start Europe's Industrial Revolution.

The slaves on plantations often lived in terrible conditions. It was so cheap to buy new slaves that overseers sometimes felt it was cheaper to work them to death, and then replace them, than it was to give them enough food and comfortable living condi-

tions. Violence was common, and slaves might expect to be whipped or beaten by the overseer if they stepped out of line. The slaves spent hours on end in the hot sun, bent almost double, hacking away at the sugarcane with machetes. The heat was terrible, and there was always danger from huge cane rats and snakes. When the plantation was busy, slaves would be out in the fields from sunrise to sunset.

Sometimes, though, slaves were allowed their own plots of land for growing food, and were treated in a kinder way. The land must have been useful, since a British House of Commons paper admitted in 1790 that the slaves' food allowance was "*of a bare sufficiency for their survival*." In some parts of the Caribbean, particularly Jamaica, slaves had a flourishing economy. Women brought any spare produce they had grown to sell at markets in the main towns.

The Middle Passage

This is the name given to the transport of slaves from the west coast of Africa to the Caribbean. It comes from the fact that this was the middle part of the three-way voyage from Europe to Africa, from Africa to the Americas, and from the Americas to Europe again. This is called the triangular trade.

Often the slaves had been captured by other Africans in raids on their homes or in wars. They were marched to the coast to be sold to European slave traders. The slaves were imprisoned on the coast, sometimes for months, until a ship came to transport them. Many of them did not survive the journey. Sharks often followed the slavers across the Atlantic, hoping to feast on the bodies. If the slavers decided that they wouldn't get enough for a slave who weakened during the voyage, he or she might be thrown overboard alive. Then the slavers could say that a slave had died during the voyage, and claim insurance money. Many times, slaves threw themselves overboard, preferring the sharks to the slavers.

To fit as many slaves as possible on board, they were kept in the most crowded and uncomfortable conditions imaginable. The slaves were forced to lie down in a cramped space, with barely enough room to move. In these conditions, diseases like dysentery flourished.

The slaves got little exercise. If the weather was good, they would be taken out on deck each day and forced to leap up and down in the air, so that their muscles did not waste away. This was called "dancing the slaves." The slavers did this so that they would still get a good price for their slaves when they were sold in the Americas.

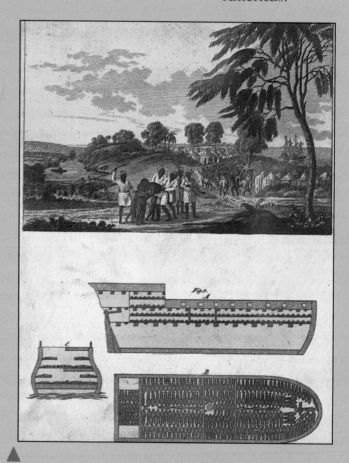

▲ (Top) Slaves are caught in Africa. (Bottom) Plan of the cramped conditions on a slave ship.

A few slaves managed
to escape and hide in
the hills. These caves in
Cuba were home to
escaped slaves.

Slaves on a sugar
plantation, where most
slaves had to work.
Often they spent all day
in the scorching sun,
working on the
sugarcane.

MAROONS

Some slaves managed to escape from the plantations into the mountainous areas in the heart of the islands. Here there were communities of escaped slaves called Maroons. The bush was thick in the mountains, and it was hard for the slave owners to get a force together to go and capture the Maroons, so they were mostly left alone. In the hills, the maroons grew their own food, and kept alive many of their African traditions. Sometimes, on the plains, the slaves must have heard the faint sound of drumming coming down to them from the wooded hills.

An escaped slave who was caught could expect to be treated very cruelly: he or she might be hung, whipped terribly, or tortured.

Maroon communities were more common in the hills of Jamaica, Hispaniola, and the Windward Islands, which had large areas of wooded hill country. On Barbados and the Leeward Islands, there were no mountainous interiors, so it was harder to find anywhere to live that was safe from the slavers.

EMANCIPATION

Between 1807 and 1863, the British, French, and Dutch passed laws that first made the international trade in slaves illegal, then outlawed slavery itself. After 1807 the British Navy began boarding ships suspected of carrying slaves and setting them free. Since the British had the most powerful navy in the world, this made it very difficult for any other country to carry on a trade in slaves.

Many ex-slaves went up into the hills where the Maroons lived. There they farmed small plots of land, which they cleared of forest. In Jamaica in 1840 (seven years after slavery had been abolished in the British West Indies), there were only 900 small holdings of under ten acres in size. By 1845 the number had increased by over twenty times, to more than 20,000. In the Caribbean today, people still live on small plots of land in the hills, growing enough food to feed themselves and perhaps a little more to sell at the market.

Freedom! Plantation slaves are told that they have been set free.

A hill farmer in the Caribbean today.

The abolition of slavery

Colonial European powers ended slavery on the following dates:

Britain   **1807** trading in slaves made illegal; **1833** slavery itself abolished.

France   **1848** slavery had briefly been abolished before, after the revolution of 1789. The second revolt on Haiti began in 1802 because it was feared that slavery would be restored there, as it had been elsewhere.

Holland   **1863**

Spain   **1873** in Puerto Rico, **1886** in Cuba. The Spanish freed slaves on Puerto Rico earlier because it was felt that slave labor was not as essential to tobacco growing as it was to sugar. Sugar was Cuba's main crop.

INDENTURED LABORERS ARRIVE

It was not long before so many ex-slaves had left the plantations that there was a great shortage of workers. Many of the plantations were bought by large companies such as Tate and Lyle, which still produces sugar for sale all around the world and owns large tracts of land in the Caribbean. To solve their labor problems, the companies began to import workers from other parts of the world. These workers were known as indentured laborers. They signed papers in their homelands to work for a long time—usually five or seven years. At the end of that time, they would be paid a sum of money and could either return to their homes or stay in the Caribbean.

Many of the indentured laborers were either Chinese or Indian. The Indians were brought mainly to Trinidad, and to a lesser extent Jamaica, Martinique, and Guadeloupe. The Chinese went mainly to Cuba.

Later, during the twentieth century, immigrants came to the Caribbean from China, Portugal, Syria, and Lebanon. These groups settled mostly in the towns, while the Indian communities remained largely in small rural farming areas.

Slaves on a coffee plantation. When slavery ended, the plantation owners were desperate for new workers. They began to bring laborers from other parts of the world.

·CARIBBEAN· ·LIFESTYLES·

*A*lthough little trace is left of the native Indians, every other group that has come to the Caribbean has added something to its music, cooking, religion, or some other part of the island culture. European settlers, slaves from West Africa, Chinese, East Indians, Portuguese, Syrians, Lebanese, and, most recently, modern American culture have all come together in the Caribbean.

COUNTRY LIFE

The rhythm of country life in the Caribbean is slow: the heat makes speed impossible. People farm small plots of land in the hills—a legacy from the days after slavery when all the land on the plains was occupied by huge plantations.

There are still agricultural projects of a similar size to the old plantations. Some are owned by multinational companies that first became rich in the days of slavery and indenture. These large landowners sometimes find it hard to find labor. The memory of slavery means that people are still unwilling to work on large agricultural projects.

The only exception to this is in Cuba, where the government has large sugarcane farms. The sugar earns Cuba valuable foreign currency, which from the 1960s to the 1980s was exchanged with Iron Curtain countries for manufactured goods. Large herds of cattle, unusual elsewhere in the Caribbean, are also found on Cuba.

Extremes of poverty and wealth have survived beyond slavery. The poverty of part of Port-au-Prince, Haiti, contrasts sharply with a wealthy suburb in the U.S. Virgin Islands.

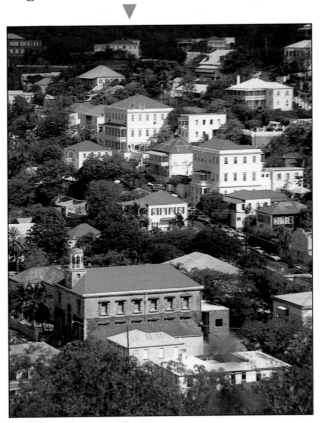

MARKETS

Small farmers try to sell anything they have to spare. It is mainly women who take goods to market: another legacy of slavery. If they are lucky, the women—some of whom have started large businesses with the profits of their market trading—will find wealthy tourists to sell their goods to. Tourists can be charged a higher price than local people.

DRUGS

Growing and selling drugs is a potential source of income for people with small plots of land up in the hills. Drugs are a major source of argument in the Caribbean. On one side are the U.S. authorities, who are desperate to stop drugs from South and Central America and the Caribbean reaching the U.S. On the other side are people in critical need of money to improve their standard of living (Excluding Bermuda, the Bahamas, and the Cayman Islands, the three richest Caribbean nations, the average income for each person in the Caribbean in 1991 was just over $3,000.)

Caught between the two extremes are the governments of the Caribbean countries. The government of Haiti, for example, realizes that its citizens are desperately poor. Corrupt officials are also sometimes willing to overlook drug smuggling—for a fee. On the other hand, Haiti is in great need of foreign aid from the U.S., which will not help if it feels that the Haitians are not doing enough to combat drug smuggling. Also, because of Haiti's political instability, its government may simply be unable to cope with the drug problem.

The result of this can sometimes be that people growing small amounts of marijuana in the hill country are raided by the police to set an example to the U.S. Big-time drug lords, who can afford to bribe government officials, get away free.

◀ *A man's head pokes up above a field of illegal marijuana plants.*

Brilliant colors in the bustle of the market on the small island of Grenada. Women, in particular, are successful market traders, and many have started large businesses with their trading profits.

TOWN LIFE

Wealthier Caribbeans rarely choose to live in the middle of town. Instead they prefer the cooler hills outside the hot cities. They have swimming pools in their backyards and air-conditioning systems to protect them from the worst of the heat.

The centers of Caribbean cities are different. The people who live there have less money and have fans in their rooms instead of expensive air-conditioning systems. The poorest people do not even have running water. Because well-paid jobs in the Caribbean are hard to come by, often the only ways people can provide for themselves is by part-time work, buying and selling goods on the street, or dealing in drugs and crime.

MUSIC

One way in which people have escaped from the poverty of the Caribbean's cities is through music. There are many distinctive kinds of music, most of which have their origins in a combination of African, European, and South American styles.

In Jamaica in the 1950s and 1960s, African and European music fused together to create ska. Stars such as the Ethiopians, Desmond Decker, and Toots and the Maytals became famous playing at open-air parties. They made records for Kong, Blue Mountain, or other small record labels. Ska music evolved a slower beat and became reggae. Reggae—like ska before it—remained a style of music that few people outside the Caribbean region listened to until a band called the Wailers appeared on the scene. The Wailers' lead singer, Bob Marley, became very famous. Today, reggae is the dance music of choice for many young people; currently popular is a variety known as dancehall, which blends elements of rap music and reggae.

▲
A steel band playing for tourists on the beach in the Bahamas.

Bob Marley

Bob Marley, the most famous reggae musician in the world.

A statue of the star stands at the end of Marley Street in Kingston, the Jamaican capital.

Bob Marley was and still is a hero to many Jamaicans, though he died in 1981. A boy from the rough, poor area of Kingston called Trenchtown, he was the lead singer of a band he set up with two friends, Bunny Wailer and Peter Tosh.

As well as being great musicians, releasing songs such as "No Woman No Cry" and "I Shot the Sheriff," Bob Marley and the Wailers were ambassadors for their religion, Rastafarianism. It was the Wailers who first made the Rastafarians'

distinctive dreadlocks famous around the world.

Near the end of his life, Marley became an important political figure in Jamaica. Throughout the 1970s, Jamaica's two main political parties, the PNP (People's National Party) and JLP (Jamaica Labor Party) were led by Michael Manley and Edward Seaga. The fierce political rivalry between the two was matched and exceeded by the confrontations between their supporters. Every election time there would be

violence and murder as the two camps raided each others' territory.

At a famous concert at election time in Jamaica, Marley brought Manley and Seaga together on stage with him. His popularity with the supporters of both parties was so great that this show of unity led to a decrease in the violence. People saw that despite their differences, they shared a love of music.

Brilliant costumes at the Junkanoo Festival, New Providence Island, the Bahamas.

Calypso King

Of all calypsonians, Mighty Sparrow is the most famous and possibly the best. For years he has thrilled audiences at the Carnival-time calypso festival in Port-of-Spain, Trinidad. Sparrow is at his best when his skills are under attack from another singer, and his cleverly worded songs have often made his rivals look foolish.

There is another, less pleasant side to calypso. Its singers rarely have a positive word to say about women, who are seen as being inferior to men. Recently, things have started to change, though, and some of the newest and most popular calypsonians are women. They don't take very happily to being thought of as inferior. Many of their songs are about what fools men are, especially men who sing calypso.

A calypso singer at a competition on the island of Dominica.

In Trinidad and Tobago, and the smaller islands nearby, calypso is popular. Every February, during Carnival, the celebrations are combined with a calypso festival. There is an official competition, with finals held on the last Sunday of the Carnival in one of Port-of-Spain's main parks, but the finest performances often take place in the unofficial tents. These spring up on almost any spare bit of ground, and inside them, on most nights, the calypsonians compete with each other for the crowd's approval. The atmosphere is intense, and the tents get incredibly hot and crowded when a famous singer is about to reveal his newest song. This is likely to be about either how great he is or how bad all his rivals are. People drink beer and rum, dance, and shout to each other over the noise, giving their views on the singer's performance.

On other islands, a more South American style is popular, especially soka (or soca) and salsa. In the 1940s and 1950s, Cuban musicians moved to Miami and New York, as well as other American cities. They took with them mambo and other Caribbean musical styles, which quickly became popular in nightclubs.

FOOD

Another area of Caribbean life that shows the blending of different cultures is the food people eat. Hot, spicy food like that of West Africa is popular, and can easily be bought on the streets and in restaurants. Curries, a legacy of the Indian indentured laborers, are common. Chinese food is also popular. Each of these cooking styles has been influenced by the other, and people no longer eat just the sort of food that is traditionally associated with their own ethnic group. Afro-Caribbeans sometimes eat Chinese food, and Chinese-Caribbean people may eat Indian food, for example.

In tourist resorts, the food is sometimes predictable international cuisine: swordfish and beef steaks, paté, roast meat, and so on. But only a few steps outside the hotel grounds, tourists may find some of the most varied and tasty food in the world.

Caraway, turmeric, chilis, and coconut among a selection of Caribbean flavorings.

▼

Cricket and Baseball in the Caribbean

The first recorded cricket match was played in Sussex, England for a bet of 50 guineas in 1697. The game had almost certainly been played for years before, and by the eighteenth century it was a refined and popular summer sport in England.

As the British Empire spread over one-fifth the world's landmass in the eighteenth and nineteenth centuries, Englishmen took their national summer sport to India, South Africa, Sri Lanka, Pakistan, Australia, and the Caribbean. These countries now have top international cricket teams.

▲
Brian Lara, who in 1994 set a record for the greatest number of runs scored in a single first-class innings, is one of many great Caribbean cricketer players.

Equally popular in the Caribbean is baseball. Baseball is the national sport in Cuba, the Dominican Republic, and other countries. Prior to the communist revolution in 1959, American baseball players routinely played exhibition games in Cuba, or played for Cuban teams. Today, according to *The Sporting News*, Cuba has developed the most powerful national baseball team in the world.

Many famous baseball players are Caribbean natives, including such Hall of Fame members as Roberto Clemente, who was born in Puerto Rico, and Juan Marichal, who was born in the Dominican Republic. For some, baseball is a means of escape from poverty. Some Cuban players defect to the United States to pursue high-paying careers in the American baseball leagues.

Fishermen on Treasure Beach, Jamaica. Fishing is an important Caribbean industry.

During the time of slavery, almost all the Caribbean islands were dependent on exporting raw material, such as sugar, tobacco, and molasses. Expensive manufactured goods were imported from abroad—usually from the European country that had colonized the island.

This trend continues today, but each island has tried different ways to break out of the system. Cuba has broken away from the United States by adopting a communist system under Fidel Castro. Puerto Rico has gone a different route, accepting help from the U.S. to build up its economy. Jamaica has followed both paths. By looking in more detail at these islands, and at one other— Haiti, one of the poorest countries in the world—it is possible to get a good idea of what the different countries of the Caribbean are like.

Caribbean economies†

Country	$ GDP/head	Annual Growth*	Area m²	Population (1991)
The Bahamas	11,750	1.3	5,380	259,000
Barbados	6,630	1.3	166	258,000
Cuba	n/a	n/a	44,218	10,736,000
Grenada	2,180	n/a	133	91,000
Haiti	370	–2.4	10,714	6,600,000
Jamaica	1,380	0.0	4,411	2,400,000
Puerto Rico	6,320	0.9	3,459	3,600,000
Trinidad and Tobago	3,670	–5.2	1,980	1,300,000
United States	22,240	1.7	3,536,341	252,700,000

GDP (Gross Domestic Product—or, the value of all goods and services produced by each country) is for 1991

*GNP per capita average annual growth, 1980-91.

†Source: World Bank, World Development Report, 1993.

These figures show a great difference in wealth between countries. The GDP of Haiti is 30 times less than that of the Bahamas, which is almost twice that of Puerto Rico.

HAITI

Haiti, the western part of the island of Hispaniola, is the poorest nation in the Western Hemisphere. It is a desolate land. Although once heavily forested, there are few other natural resources. Even these have been mostly used up, either by colonists, foreign companies, or greedy government officials.

Pressure on the land from uncontrolled use has led to severe soil erosion. In the past, coffee and sugar were valuable crops for the Haitian economy but since the late 1970s the country imports more sugar than it exports. Some hillsides are bare, especially north and south of Port au Prince, the capital, and the northwest of the country. Because

◄

A Haitian boy balances bananas on his head. Most people in Haiti are farmers.

35

there is so little commercial agricultural work, many farmers concentrate on growing the food they can eat themselves - corn, rice, beans, and vegetables. If they have any spare produce they can try to make money by selling it at small roadside stands. The average monthly income in Haiti in 1991 was $31. Because this is an average figure, some people earned more than $31 but a great many earned less.

There is little manufacturing industry in Haiti. Most industry now involves labor-intensive work such as making clothing and sporting goods, which is exported for sale, mostly to the United States. There are gold, copper, and bauxite reserves but everything in Haiti is over-shadowed by the political situation. Violence and corruption have been common. This means foreign businesses do not want to risk money or equipment in Haiti. And the Haitians do not have the means to mine and process the ore themselves.

The people of Haiti have been at the mercy of colonial government or dictators for hundreds of years and it is only very recently that democracy is being attempted. It will take some time to tell if it is a success for the country, the people, and the economy.

▲
Trying to sell extra produce at the market in Port-au-Prince, Haiti's capital.

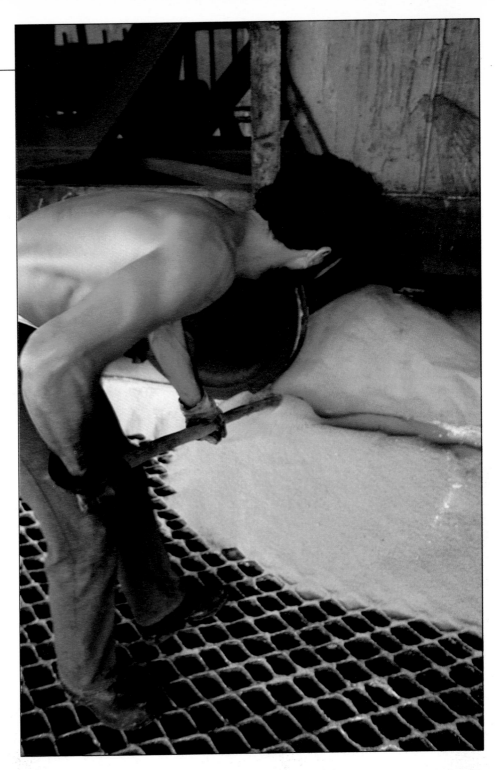

A Cuban sugar worker. Farming sugarcane requires very hard labor under difficult conditions, and most people understandably dislike it. Cuba, though, is desperate to earn foreign currency, which it can do from the sale of sugar.

CUBA

In the 1950s Cuba, like Puerto Rico, had a very close relationship with the United States. When the communist government came to power in Cuba in 1959, however, toppling the dictator Fulgencio Batista, the new leader, Fidel Castro, rejected the U.S. in favor of closer links with the U.S.S.R. Cuba relied on being able to trade such goods as sugar and tobacco with the European communist countries. Most of Cuba's oil, for example, came from the U.S.S.R.

Tourism in Cuba

A new hotel being built in Varadero, Cuba.

Since subsidies for the Cuban economy from the U.S.S.R. have stopped, the Cuban government has been desperately short of cash with which to buy goods on the international market. One area it has targeted for raising more revenue is tourism. Cubans aim to attract a million tourists to the island in 1995. They have begun a program of hotel building, and now allow package tours from capitalist countries to bring tourists to Cuba.

So far tourism has brought a significant boost to the Cuban economy. In 1990, 340,000 arrivals generated an income of $250 million. In the first quarter of 1991 arrivals were up 20 percent over the previous year and earnings from tourism had gone up 39 percent. Part of the increase was accounted for by Cuba playing host to the 1991 Pan-American Games, which brought 20,000 visitors to Havana, the capital.

The U.S. trade embargo meant that U.S. television companies were not able to pay the Cuban government an estimated $9 million to televise the games. So the government let the American stations televise the games for free.

Cuban soils are very rich. Sugar is the main crop, as it has been since the eighteenth century, but rice and citrus fruit – an important export – are also common. Tobacco, some of which goes into the famous Havana cigars, is another major crop. Fishing provides Cubans with a large part of the protein in their diet.

Cuba has little manufacturing industry. About half its industry is related to agriculture. Food processing, tobacco, and soft drink and beer production are the main agricultural industries. Cuba has a small oil industry which fills only half the country's needs, and there are also construction, chemical, and clothing industries.

One of Cuba's main resources is its beauty. It has the sandy beaches, sunshine, and relaxed lifestyle that have made other islands into popular tourist resorts. Tourists from the U.S. have required special permission to go to Cuba since 1961, when the U.S. broke off relations with Cuba after U.S. investments and landholdings were seized. The Cuban government is eager to encourage tourism. After the breakup of the U.S.S.R., subsidies from eastern Europe for the Cuban economy ended, and tourism brings the government desperately needed foreign currency with which to buy imported goods.

An old petrochemical factory in Puerto Rico. Now, Puerto Rico alone in the Caribbean is home to large electronics and pharmaceuticals industries.

▼

PUERTO RICO

Spain once ruled Puerto Rico, but it was occupied by the United States during the Spanish-American War in 1898. It has been a U.S. possession in the Caribbean ever since, and the majority of people on the island still support its Commonwealth status. Two small groups are in favor of an independent Puerto Rico or of the country becoming a U.S. state. Puerto Rico's fortunes are closely tied to those of the U.S.

After World War II, Operation Bootstrap was launched to develop Puerto Rico's economy. It was largely successful, and Puerto Rico is the only Caribbean island where most of the labor force is involved in industry instead of agriculture. Initially companies based on the U.S. mainland moved to the island because of the low wage rates there. The government also offered new industries tax reductions and

▲

A Puerto Rican city.

other advantages if they moved to Puerto Rico. There is a minimum wage on the island, and skilled workers and industries already are there. It is home to high-tech producers of chemicals, electronic goods, and medical equipment.

Puerto Rico's other main industry is tourism, which brings millions of dollars to the island every year. Visitors, mainly from North America, come to gamble in the casinos, bask in the sun on the beaches, and soak up the relaxed Caribbean atmosphere. The combination of tourism and developed industry means that Puerto Ricans are quite wealthy by Caribbean standards: in 1991 the average income was $6,330.

Water Sports in the Caribbean

The clear, unpolluted seas of the Caribbean attract water sports enthusiasts of all kinds: sailors, windsurfers, surfers, and divers. Windsurfing can be enjoyed, and there are groups of surfers in Puerto Rico and Barbados. There is good surf in Tobago, the Dominican Republic, and other islands, too.

The attraction to sailors is obvious: warm seas, good weather, and thousands of interesting islands to visit. Unfortunately, the Caribbean is repeating its past, when Hispaniola was a feared pirate base. In the last few years, there have been increasing numbers of attacks on tourists' boats, either for robbery or hijacking. There have even been murders.

The Caribbean is a paradise for scuba divers, who are attracted to the warm, clear sea and coral reefs crowded with fish. The Cayman Islands are one of the most developed resorts for divers, but there are other less well-known places to go. The tiny Dutch island of Saba, only five miles long, is surrounded by a reef that is a marine park for its entire length. The result is that many of the fish are tame, never having been hunted by divers, and will happily swim right up to you, hoping you will give them something to eat.

Catamarans drawn up on a Caribbean beach.

A bauxite mine in Jamaica. Bauxite is used to make aluminum. It can earn Jamaica foreign currency if the bauxite is exported or processed in Jamaica and then sold abroad.

JAMAICA

Jamaica is an independent member of the British Commonwealth, and is the third-largest Caribbean island. It has natural resources that can be exploited for profit, especially its reserves of bauxite, which is used to make aluminum. Many of these reserves were owned or mined by foreign firms, usually British or U.S. This led the government of Jamaica into confrontation with the U.S. and Britain in the late 1970s, when it tried to nationalize the mining industry. Foreign involvement in mining is now decreasing, and the government is taking a larger role.

The bauxite mines, which are usually strip mines, have damaged parts of the Jamaican environment badly. As well as the damage caused by the mines themselves—which are little more than huge holes in the ground— the water that runs from them is often badly polluted and harmful to the soils and crops it reaches. But the mines do bring employment and valuable foreign currency to Jamaica.

Agriculture is important to Jamaica: the main crops are sugar and bananas. Coffee, citrus fruit, tobacco, and cocoa are also grown. Fishing is another major employer: about 150,000 people work in the fishing industry. Most Jamaican boats fish in coastal waters, but some larger boats go as far as 300 miles away.

Tourism is also an important source of income for Jamaica.

Caribbean tourist arrivals 1990-91

Increase	Decrease
Bonaire +22%	Bahamas -10%
Aruba +19%	Bermuda -10%
Grenada +17%	Puerto Rico -10%
Trinidad and Tobago +12%	
St. Lucia +11%	

The less well-known islands are attracting more visitors as people seek out unusual places. Established tourist resorts may suffer badly. In the Bahamas, for example, January arrivals by air were down 22 percent in 1991 compared with the same month in 1990. In February the decrease was 24 percent. This had a major effect on government finances. Over the whole of the first quarter of the year in 1991 there was a decrease in tourist arrivals of 12.5 percent, which reduced the government's income by 10 percent. These figures show how dependent on tourism many of the Caribbean islands are.

▶ *Cruise ships anchored in the harbor of St. George's, Grenada.*

GRENADA

Grenada was one of the last islands to be conquered by Europeans and taken from the fierce Carib Indians. The Caribs fought off a group of British traders as late as 1609. The island did eventually end up in the hands of the British, however, and Grenada is an independent member of the British Commonwealth.

Agriculture and tourism are the biggest employers in Grenada. Even more than on other Caribbean islands, agriculture is small scale and there are few large farms. People grow a variety of crops on small plots of land. Mechanized farming is rare because farms are small and the countryside is mountainous. The main crops are cocoa, bananas, nutmeg, limes, tropical fruits, and vegetables.

One advantage of Grenada's small-scale agriculture and lack of large industry is that the island is the kind of unspoiled tropical paradise that is popular with tourists. The government has encouraged tourism. Visitors bring increasing amounts of foreign currency to Grenada. One reason for this is the success of the new airport, begun by the revolutionary Jewel government (**J**oint **E**ndeavor for **W**elfare, **E**ducation, and **L**iberation) of Maurice Bishop with the aid of Cuba in the early 1980s. But the main increase in the number of visitors comes from cruise ships. In 1984 only 34,000 passengers visited the island, but by 1992 the figure had risen to 196,000. The number of hotel rooms on Grenada is set to increase over the next few years, but most visitors are from ships, which have their own accommodations. The impact of hotel building on the local environment is not likely to be as great as elsewhere in the Caribbean, where whole skylines have been ruined by tourist hotels.

▲
A Grenadan man cutting bananas to sell.

·CONCLUSION·

▶ *A fiery sunset over Cruz Bay in the U.S. Virgin Islands. In the distance the lights of a town sparkle across the water.*

Most Caribbean countries are relatively poor. Puerto Rico has developed industry and commercial agriculture, but most islands have not. The region's environment is generally safe from the kind of damage that has occurred in the Amazon rain forests. (There, miners, loggers, and cattle ranchers are responsible for the continuing destruction of one of the world's most valuable environments.) This is because it is in the Caribbean's interest to keep its environment undamaged.

A huge proportion of the region's income is from tourism. The blue seas and sky and the beautiful landscapes bring hundreds of thousands of visitors to the region each year. The majority of the islands depend on the income these visitors bring to be able to pay for imported manufactured goods. Destruction of

the environment would have a devastating effect on the lives of the people.

Tourism has its problems, though. This year's fashionable destination may not attract as many visitors in eighteen months' time. Economic recessions in wealthy nations and political unrest also threaten tourist income. Without tourist income, many Caribbean countries could rapidly sink into the poverty that affects the people of Haiti—once a fairly wealthy Caribbean nation, now the poorest country in the northern and western hemispheres.

The challenge for the future is to develop industries that will provide jobs and are not so dependent on the whims of tourism. The Caribbean governments must try to do this without ruining the beauty that brings so many people to the Caribbean each year.

GLOSSARY

Bhangra A style of music from the Indian subcontinent, played on a mixture of traditional Indian and modern instruments. It has a very strong beat.

Calypso A song which usually refers to some current event or personality sung in a particular style.

Cay A coral or sand reef or island. The word comes from the Spanish *cayo*, meaning reef or shoal.

Cloud forest A forest high up in the mountains that is generally covered in cloud.

Communist A person who believes that it is wrong for wealth to be concentrated in the hands of a few people. Communism advocates the elimination of all private property.

Coral A small sea creature with a horny coat, or the deposits these creatures leave behind them. A coral reef is made up of millions of these deposits.

Colonialism The practice of taking over another country to make a profit. Colonialism was at its height in the nineteenth century, when the European countries took over most of the rest of the world.

Drug A substance containing chemicals that affect the human body. Drugs can be helpful—for example, painkillers for a headache. Drugs can also be harmful—if people take a drug regularly, they can become addicted to it, and are unable to behave normally without it.

Geothermal Heat from within the earth, for example, hot springs or geysers.

Grunt A tropical fish. There are different kinds, but all of them make a grunting noise when they are caught.

Indenture A contract binding one person to work for another for a set period of time, in return for payment of travel expenses and/or room and board. Many migrants to the Americas paid for their travel by making such an arrangement.

Mammal Any warm-blooded creature with a backbone and mammary glands in females. Whales, bats, rats, and cats are all mammals – so are people.

Maroon A slave who had escaped from his or her captors was known as a Maroon. "Maroon" was a derogatory name; it comes from the Spanish word *cimarón*, meaning savage or wild.

Rain forest A dense forest found in areas of high rainfall, with trees of many different heights.

Reggae A musical style that originated in Jamaica, and has a strong beat.

Soil erosion Loss of the top layer of soil, due perhaps to the wind or the rain carrying it away.

Ska A style of dance music that originated in Jamaica.

Triangular trade The trade in goods, slaves and sugar that ran between Europe, Africa, and the Americas. It was abolished in the early nineteenth century.

Anthony, Suzanne. *Haiti*. Let's Visit Places and Peoples of the World. New York: Chelsea House, 1989.

Aylesworth, Thomas G. and Aylesworth, Virginia L. *Territories and Possessions*. Let's Discover the States. New York: Chelsea House, 1992.

The Cambridge Encyclopedia of Latin America and the Caribbean. Second Edition. New York: Cambridge University Press, 1992.

Chrisp, Peter. *Spanish Conquests in the New World*. Exploration and Encounters. New York: Thomson Learning, 1993.

Hull, Robert. *Caribbean Stories*. Tales from Around the World. New York: Thomson Learning, 1994.

Lerner Geography Staff. *Jamaica in Pictures*. Visual Geography. Minneapolis: Lerner Publications, 1987.

McKenley, Yvonne. *A Taste of the Caribbean*. Food Around the World. New York: Thomson Learning, 1995.

Springer, Eintou Pearl. *The Caribbean*. Revised Edition. Morristown, NJ: Silver Burdett Press, 1987.

Useful Addresses

CARE
660 First Avenue
New York, NY 10016

Caribbean/Latin American Action
1818 N Street NW
Suite 310
Washington, DC 20036

Caribbean Tourism Organization
20 East 46th Street
New York, NY 10017

Environmental Defense Fund
1616 P Street NW
Suite 150
Washington, DC 200036

Environmental Protection Agency
401 M Street SW
Washington, DC 20460

UNICEF
3 United Nations Plaza
New York, NY 10017

United States Department of State
2201 C Street, NW
Washington, DC 20210

World Wildlife Fund
1250 24th Street NW
Washington, DC 20037

INDEX

Numbers in **bold** refer to pictures as well as text.